YOU'RE ONLY ONE DEAL AWAY

A Roadmap To Build And Scale Your Wholesale Real Estate Business

By: Edward Hayes

Edward Hayes

Copyright © 2019 by Edward Hayes

All rights reserved. No part of this publication may be reproduced, distributed, or transmitted in any form or by any means, including photocopying, recording, or other electronic or mechanical methods, without the prior written permission of the publisher, except in the case of brief quotations embodied in critical reviews and certain other noncommercial uses permitted by copyright law. For permission requests, write to the publisher, addressed "Attention: Permissions Coordinator," at the address below.

ACKNOWLEDGEMENTS:

I want to thank all of the people that made this book a reality.

To all my friends and fans that consume my content online. Thank you. You make it all worthwhile for me. You all allow me to live my best life.

To my fiance Candance, if it weren't for you, I wouldn't be who I am. You're my muse. Thank you for being patient with me during the long nights and early mornings. It'll all pay off.

To those who didn't believe in me or encouraged me to quit, thank you for giving me the fuel needed to keep grinding. One of my biggest motivations in life is not becoming you....

To my step-daughter Alex, I dedicate this book to you and your future. Seeing a smile on your face is my biggest inspiration.

And lastly, to you, the reader. Thank you for purchasing this book. I truly hope it changes your life for the better and you gain the tools necessary to dominate as a wholesaler.

Let's get into this content!

You're Only One Deal Away!

Table of Contents

Acknowledgements:	Iii
Chapter 1: Introduction: What Is Wholesaling?	1
Chapter 2: Creating A Presence Online & Offline	4
Chapter 3: Become A Concierge For Your Buyers	8
Chapter 4: Start Hunting For Inventory	14
Chapter 5: Analyzing & Viewing Properties	19
Chapter 6: Marketing Like A Pro	28
Chapter 7: Closing & Getting Paid	32
Chapter 8: Automation & Delegation	36
Chapter 9: In Conclusion	40
Chapter 10: Guides & Resources	42
How To Find Cash Buyers	42
How To Build A Massive Cash Buyers List	44
How To Become A Concierge For Buyers:	48
Compiling A List Of Motivated Sellers	53
Cold Calling Tips And Strategies	57
Cold Caller Interview Flow	62

Edward Hayes

39 Different Ways To Market Your Wholesaling Business	68
How To Skip Trace Online Free	70
** Catchy Headline That Grabs Their Attention!!! ***	72
The Wholesaling Checklist V.1	74
Ed's Hierarchy Of Wholesaling:	86
About The Author	92

CHAPTER 1:
Introduction:
What Is Wholesaling?

I'll assume you already know what wholesaling is, but in case you don't here's the definition from Investopedia:

"Real estate **wholesaling** occurs when a party (the "wholeseller") contracts with a home seller, markets the home to potential buyers, and then assigns the contract to one of them. The wholesaler makes a profit, which is the difference between the contracted price with the seller and the amount paid by the buyer."

Here's how I would define wholesaling: "Real estate wholesaling occurs when a wholesaler sells their contract to purchase a homeowner's property to an investor for a fee."

I hope that doesn't sound complex, but if it does, that's why I made this book. To break down how to actually wholesale real estate and start getting deals done.

Wholesaling has become a craze nationwide. People from all takes of life are jumping in and trying to learn the best ways to take advantage of this budding industry. There's a ton of different strategies, many of which will be discussed in this book, but there's also a ton of confusion amongst new wholesalers.

At every job you've had there's always been a trainer to teach you the ropes. Well, wholesaling is a business, and there aren't trainers out there to help people along the way. Getting a personal mentor or coach is the only real way to learn the game and know that you're playing by the rules. I started coaching people back in the winter of 2017 and since then I've gone on to help my clients earn over $1,200,000 in assignment fees. These strategies really work and they're the basis for everything I do in my business.

This isn't my first rodeo.

I've been building businesses since 2007 when I graduated from high school. I was one of those guys calling my friends asking them to sign up to be Amway Global affiliates. I've learned and grown a lot since then, but the basis of how to build a business has never changed. When I first learned about wholesaling I applied the same types of strategies I've used to build my other businesses. I didn't reinvent the wheel or do anything fancy. I've just applied the best strategies from people across the nation and implemented them into my business. This book is the distillation of 3 years of wholesaling and earning over half a million dollars personally in assignment fees. I hope this book give you all the tools necessary to dominate as a wholesaler in your market and create generational wealth for you and your family. Get ready to take MASSIVE ACTION!

CHAPTER 2:
Creating A Presence Online & Offline

First off, let's talk about your presence. The internet has made it easier than ever to research a company and see whether they're legit or if they even exist. When you first start off wholesaling, you don't have a name for yourself, you haven't done any deals and no one knows who you are. You've got to create that presence online and offline so when people go looking for you, they can actually find you and you're aware of and in control over what they see.

Note to the reader: The foundation of everything you're going to read in this book will be based in integrity and honesty. There's no need to lie to sellers or buyers or anyone else for that matter.

You're building a business and every business has to start from somewhere. Everyone is new at some point. You shouldn't try to overinflate or fabricate your wholesaling resume to impress people. This will only lead to you potentially burning bridges and being seen as deceptive.

Get a website

You can create a website using a variety of paid and free methods. One simple strategy is to go to wordpress.com or pages.google.com to create a free website. This can just be a placeholder at the beginning but you'll want to spruce it up over time. You can also go to investorcarrot.com to get a great website created for about $50 at the time of writing this. Whichever option you choose, just make sure that you add tags and keywords to your site to make it easier for search engines to find it. You may want to consider hiring someone to get this setup for you if you're not tech savvy at all, but don't spend your whole marketing budget on it.

Get some business cards made

Most of the people you'll be interacting with will come from an older generation. They did things differently in their days. One of those things was having business cards with you as a way for people to stay in contact with you. I highly recommend that you get yourself some business cards made at vistaprint.com before beginning your journey.

Business cards are great for making sure the people you encounter remember who you are. You can leave them everywhere too. At the gym, at gas stations, at your school, wherever you can place them legally is a great place to leave them. They can help you start to generate some calls and ensure you have something to give to everyone you encounter.

Get a logo and business email address

A custom logo and business email address is a great way to start branding yourself online to stand out from the competition. You can get a logo created at Fiverr.com for as little as $5, so try not to overspend for this simple expense.

To get a business email address, I'd recommend using GoDaddy and purchasing your custom domain name, then during the checkout process you'll have the option to add an email address to your order.

Do you need an LLC?

People ask this all the time when they're starting off. You do not need an LLC to wholesale houses. However it can help you gain more credibility. When used in combination with the before mentioned ways to establish your presence, it's a great way to look professional.

If you're going to get an LLC I would recommend using a P.O Box as your business mailing address so as to not have people coming to your house.

JUST START

One of the most common things I see wholesalers struggling with is simply taking action. Many people will know everything they need to do and simply never take action. If you want to be successful as a wholesaler, just start taking action after reading this book. You don't have to overthink or overanalyze. Experience in the game of wholesaling is the best teacher and you can never learn if you sit on the sidelines.

CHAPTER 3:
Become A Concierge For Your Buyers

In my opinion, building your cash buyers list is the most critical part of creating the foundation of your business. Every business needs customers.

Hopefully Wholesaling

If you're going out to seller's houses telling them you're going to buy their houses and you haven't established relationships with investors in your area, that's just being disingenuous. Many "gurus" out there teach this and other deceptive wholesaling strategies. This typically leads to a lot of time wasted by all parties involved *especially* when the wholesaler is brand new. You don't want your contracts to constantly expire because you don't have buyers interested in your properties.

You're Only One Deal Away!

This is what I call "Hopefully Wholesaling". Hopefully someone will want to buy this. Hopefully the contract won't expire. Hopefully this is a good area buyers are looking to buy in. This Hopefully Wholesaling is the reason why 90% of "wholesalers" aren't making any money. That's simply not the way you run a business.

Actually Wholesaling

Businesses start with target market research. They want to know what they're customers are buying, how much, where, and how they can help their customers accomplish their goals. In a wholesale deal the customer is the buyer. They have the resources to fund these deals and they're the one coming to the closing table with a check. When you're actually wholesaling properties you'll realize that without a buyer, no one's getting paid.

You've got to reach out to these buyers and find out what they're looking for. I've got a ton of strategies on exactly what to say and how to say it later on in the book, but for now, we'll talk about the reason for doing this.

The Roadmap to Dealflow

When you talk to cash buyers you are trying to find out exactly what they're looking for. I like to position myself as a concierge for my buyers. In other words, I want each of them to feel like I'm catering to them by bringing them specifics investments they're most likely to be interested in. The script that I use is in the back of the book for you to take advantage of.

When you figure out what investors in your area are looking for you get much better target market research than average wholesalers. Going directly to the source means you have the information needed to confidently determine price points, locations and probability to close. A property that fits the criteria for multiple buyers on your list is much more likely to close than a property that no one has told you they're interested in.

This upfront knowledge of your market is going to be the key to getting multiple deals per month and scaling quickly. When you're doing a wholesale deal you want to be representing your buyers. You need to know what they want and how they like to invest to be able to serve them best. This is the roadmap to dealflow. When you're working on behalf of multiple investors in a given area, you're able to walk into a seller's house with confidence that you can get it sold for them. The buyers have confidence in you knowing

You're Only One Deal Away!

you're bringing them exactly what they're looking for. The deal goes through because you genuinely are the solution to the buyer and seller's problems. You're a wholesaler, a matchmaker, and most importantly a problem solver.

Where To Start Looking

Where to find cash buyers is one of the most common questions I get asked by newbie wholesalers. Here's a few recommendations for finding them online:

1. Gosection8.com
2. Forrentbyowner.com
3. Listsource.com
4. Craigslist.org
5. Freedomsoft
6. Propstream
7. https://www.motivatedsellerleads.org

If you want to use offline resources to generate cash buyer leads, here are some of my best offline methods:

1. Bandit Signs
2. Flyers
3. Business Cards
4. Stickers

5. Direct Mail
6. REIA Meetings
7. Property/Tax Auctions

These are some of my favorite resources for generating cash buyer leads online and offline. You can reach out to them using a variety of marketing strategies which will be discussed later in this book.

The Value Of It All

This process, building your cash buyers list, establishing relationships, and gathering criteria is a never ending process. This is one of the most vital pieces to a successful wholesaling business. As the saying goes, "It's not what you know, it's who you know." Having relationships with serious investors in your area will give you a leg up above your competition.

You'll also become a valuable asset to not only investors, but other wholesalers as well who have properties they need help closing on. Becoming an asset to investors makes you an indispensable part of the real estate market in your area.

You're Only One Deal Away!

Investors need people who can go out and analyze a deal and take some of that load off their shoulders.

When you provide value to your investors they in turn provide value to the community and it starts a snowball of positive effects. If you're serious about your wholesaling business you'll want to get to know every serious investor in your area. You want to know what they're looking for, what are their outlooks for the year and how you can help them accomplish their goals.

I talk about the value of it all because so many wholesalers at the beginning are just so eager to go view properties and start making offers. The true value you provide to a seller is based on your likelihood of being able to help them sell their home. If you haven't taken the time to strategically build and segment your cash buyers list, you're not quite ready to start looking for properties. Be patient and play the long game. I truly believe that most wholesalers fail because they look at wholesaling as a way to make a some quick cash and put that money into something else their interested in. If you're willing to take the time necessary to genuinely strive to provide value for the investors and the sellers you'll never want for money

DON'T RUSH THROUGH THIS PROCESS LIKE MOST PEOPLE DO!

What To Do With The Info

Once you've compiled your buyer's criteria you need to segment the buyers into different categories that make sense to you. For instance if you have three buyers who mention they want brick single family homes in a particular county and another group of buyers interested in multi-families. Or you may have a group that only wants light repairs and another who prefers big projects. You may want to sort your buy and hold investors out from your flippers. Once you've segmented your buyers list you'll start to build your list of motivated seller leads that match their criteria.

CHAPTER 4:
Start Hunting For Inventory

So you've gotten your buyer's criteria and you're ready to start finding deals for them. This is where the pedal hits the medal. This is also where most wholesalers start to get confused and analysis paralysis kicks in. Applying the tools and resources in this book will allow you to replicate my process of finding and analyzing deals in a short time.

Let's talk about finding motivated sellers. The best thing about wholesaling real estate is that there's a never ending supply of inventory. There are homeowners around the country that need to sell their homes and you get paid for matching investors with sellers. The market conditions do not affect our business model.

I just want to mention that all of the marketing strategies we'll discuss will require time, effort and very often money to implement. Don't expect to be an overnight success if you're just starting off. Give yourself modest goals based on your own abilities and resources. If you're in this for the long haul it doesn't matter where you are in relation to others. You've got to be willing to keep trying and adjusting along the way to get the best results.

Here are some of my favorite ways to finding motivated sellers:

1. https://www.motivatedsellerleads.org
2. Propstream
3. REWW
4. Listsource
5. Local county websites
6. All The Leads (Probate Leads)
7. Facebook Ads
8. Google Ads
9. Driving For Dollars
10. Flyers and Bandit Signs
11. Direct Mail

My favorite ways to generate leads are driving for dollars and getting lists online. I keep a steady stream of leads coming in utilizing both methods. My favorite site to use is https://www.motivatedsellerleads.org. They make it really nice and easy to get a list by simply filling out a form then customizing your order. You can add skip tracing onto your order as well to get the homeowner's contact information.

You're Only One Deal Away!

The rest of my strategies to generate motivated seller leads will be listed in the back of this book as well as how to approach these sellers.

You'll want to gather separate lists for your different groups of buyers. Once you've gathered your lists you'll need to get the homeowner's contact information so you can begin to market to them.

Here are my favorite resources to get homeowner contact info:

1. https://www.motivatedsellerleads.org
2. Truepeoplesearch.com
3. Fastpeoplesearch.com
4. Beenverified.com
5. Propstream
6. DealMachine
7. Landglide

If you plan to gather the contact information yourself, I recommend truepeoplesearch.com. The site is completely free and it only takes about 60 seconds to get the homeowner's contact information online. If you're driving for dollars I highly recommend DealMachine to gather and organize your leads. If you want to let someone else skip trace your leads for you I recommend https://www.motivatedsellerleads.org.

As you can tell, there are a ton of options for sourcing leads and gathering their contact information. You have to choose the systems that work best with your abilities and resources. After you've found a lead and found their contact information it's time to start making some phone calls.

Cold Calling Motivated Sellers

When you're cold calling homeowners it's important to keep in mind you're trying to help them. Don't see them as a paycheck. Try to do more listening and less talking. Your goal is to help them solve a problem that they have. This is where having cash buyers in place already makes a big difference. You'll be much more confident knowing you have someone who's interested in this area and for a property like the one you're calling. That confidence shines through the phone as you speak.

Try not to talk price over the phone if you don't have to. Don't ask any questions about how much they want for the property or how much they think it's worth. You'll get anchored at whatever price they throw out, and most sellers aren't experts on home values.

You'll get all the details from them over the phone and find out their motivation for selling still, but don't talk price over the phone. From my own results and the results of others nationwide, I can tell you with certainty, you'll have drastically higher conversion rates in person than over the phone or text or email. The personal touch makes the whole difference.

THE MAIN PURPOSE OF THE PHONE CALL IS TO MAKE AN APPOINTMENT WITH THE SELLER TO VIEW THE PROPERTY

When talking to the seller you want to be building rapport with them and getting to know them better. Find out why their trying to sell and why they haven't listed it with a realtor. Get a general sense of the repairs needed inside. Confirm the amount of beds and baths. Ask them what features made them buy the house. Be sure to get their contact information before you get off the phone with them and call them by name as often as possible. Make sure you move around while talking to keep your energy levels up. Mirror their tonalities and most importantly, smile. Smiling while on the phone can be felt by the listener on the other end. You come off as joyful and likeable. These are just some of my cold calling strategies. There are tons more in the back of this book to help you along the way.

Once you've found someone is ready to sell, you'll need to know how to analyze their property to know whether it's a deal or not.

CHAPTER 5:
Analyzing & Viewing Properties

Like I said in the previous chapter, there's a never ending supply of properties you can choose from to find your deals. However you have to sort through the non-deals to get to the good ones. What most wholesalers do is jump on each and every opportunity that comes their way. You find out quickly that a lot of people want to sell their homes, but most homes for sale aren't "deals". Investors are looking for those diamond in the rough properties that no one else has or that are unique from the others in the community. And trust me they're looking for them. The active investors in your community will know exactly what they're looking for and where and how much they want to spend. They can walk into a property and within minutes come up with an offer. That's why having your investor partners already locked in is going to be crucial at this step.

At the property you'll want to pay attention to a variety of things concerning the condition of the property. Those things include but are not limited to:

a. Foundation
b. Roof
c. Mechanicals
d. Windows
e. Flooring
f. Room Sizes
g. Floor Plans
h. Kitchen/bath conditions
i. Anything else that looks like it needs updating, repair or replacing

Be sure to get very good pictures and video of the entire property (every square inch!). The better the video and picture quality, the more likely you'll have people interested in making offers and viewing the property. Put these pics and video in a Google Drive or iCloud or Dropbox folder and make the link shareable. This way you can easily share the link to the images and videos of the property with potential buyers.

Be sure also to bring a lockbox with you to the property. If you and the seller agree on terms at the property you can ask them to leave a copy of the key at the property in the lockbox for you and your partners to get back in to get estimates.

The general calculation for determining your offer is ARV X .70 - Repairs - Your Assignment Fee = Your Max Allowable Offer

I try not to get stuck in equations and prefer to know the market that I'm in and know what the investors really want to pay for a given property in a given area.

There's no one right way to calculate your offers on a property. However, the most common way I see investors determine how much they want to pay is based on what other homes have sold for in the area recently. You can use sites like Realtor.com to determine what homes are selling for in a given zip code. I like to look from the low end to the high end houses and determine a general market value from low to high. This is what properties are selling for in the area.

Remember, you've already got a roadmap provided by your investors. Every property you go see should be within their criteria. So after you've viewed a property, I sometimes like to soft-shop a property to my closest buyers. By soft-shopping I mean asking them how much they think this property is worth and how much they would be willing to spend on it. I don't include the property address or any of the owner's info. I just tell them a general area and the property specs. Gather as much feedback about the property as possible in the initial stages. I've often-times received multiple offers on a property even before I've put it under contract. But I AM NOT suggesting you start full-on marketing properties you do not have under contract. And I would not suggest you imply that you have it under contract already to your buyers. You're simply looking for some feedback about a property you may have coming into the pipeline.

Analyzing these deals takes some time and expertise. You absolutely need to know your market to be most effective. The easiest way to gather this market knowledge is to build relationships with the people who're buying the real estate. Sometimes analyzing a deal is as simple as shooting a text to your buyer and asking how much and having them text you back with a number. Then you would just go get the property under contract for less than what you know you have a buyer willing to spend. That's reverse engineering the deal.

Here is a list of resources you can use to analyze your deals and find out what properties are selling for in the area:

1. Propstream
2. Realtor.com
3. REWW.com

4. A Relationship With A Realtor
5. A Relationship With An Active Investor

As you can see the list is short, because I don't need to use too many resources to get this information. Price is a very subjective topic, meaning if you ask ten different people what they think a property is worth you'll ten different answers. So don't stress out trying to figure every little thing out. Keep in mind that the range that properties are selling for in an area. Typically if you can put a property under contract for less than the average sales price in an area, you can get a deal done.

My number one way to analyze properties is Propstream. It allows you to enter the property address and instantly have all the information you need to quickly analyze a property and determine its value. It has a ton of other features as well to help you determine rental estimates, mortgage amounts, owner information, comparables, repair estimates and so much more. I use Propstream on a daily basis in my business and its helped us scale our business tremendously since we added it to our funnel. It has marketing features built-in like skip tracing, direct mail campaigns and ringless voicemail drops. It's an indispensable tool in the wholesaler's toolbox in my opinion.

Once you've analyzed the property and you've determined whether it's a deal or not, it's time to start making offers.

Making Offers

As a wholesaler, you make your money when you put the property under contract. The buyer will only be willing to spend so much more than the price you get the property under contract for. Your offer needs to make sense to the buyer and the seller and everyone must be getting a good deal to have the highest chance of closing on the property. Keep this in mind. In an assignment deal everything is disclosed to both the seller and buyer. Everyone will be aware how much money you're making, how much you got it under contract for and how much you're assigning it for. And everyone has to sign off on that and be okay with everyone's cut.

The Dark Side

This is the dark side of wholesaling many people don't talk about. These deals collapse at the closing table all the time when wholesalers are trying to get rich off of one deal. The sellers often get upset about how much the wholesaler is making or unexpected expenses like taxes owed come up last minute and destroy the hopes of a deal going through. Keep this in mind when making offers.

You're Only One Deal Away!

Taxes

If the property owes taxes on it, these are typically paid for by the buyer in a wholesale deal. As well as any other costs associated with closing the property if the sales amount is very low. If the sales amount is high ($50,000 or more) the seller will likely be expected to pay any property taxes, liens or other fees associated with closing the property. If your buyer will be paying the taxes on the property, I typically add these costs into the sale price.

Try to get the property under contract for as low as possible! This is not the time to try to "be nice" or try to give extra money to make sure that the seller is happy. You need to make sure you get the property at a price low enough to attract several buyers in the area. If your buyers offer a significantly higher amount than what you were expecting you can always give them extra money on the deal. But going back to renegotiate after you've gotten the property under contract can often be a headache and can potentially ruin the deal.

Earnest Money

If a seller is looking for an earnest money deposit, this fee can be paid for by your buyer. If you have to put up the money yourself because you don't have a buyer yet, try to negotiate that price to be $100 or less. You don't want to be putting up your own money in a wholesale deal. Most sellers won't be looking for an earnest money deposit if they're really motivated. Some of them will if they were burned by wholesalers in the past or they have a lot of real estate experience. YOU should always require a non-refundable EMD from your buyer upon signing your assignment contract. If they fail to perform you not only get the earnest money for your seller, you get paid as well. I typically require $2,500 down for any contract I'm assigning.

Contracts

What contracts should you be using is a very common question I get from my coaching clients. I recommend reaching out to title companies and attorneys in your local area that are familiar with wholesaling and asking them for their contracts. This way you know they will be well versed in their own contract and can provide you guidance on filling it out if needed. I suggest you ask for recommendations on Facebook to find wholesale friendly title companies and attorneys in your area.

You're Only One Deal Away!

I also have the same contracts I use to get deals nationwide available on my website at https://www.edwardhayes.org/Contracts.

I use a variety of contracts depending on the situation I'm in. I have a special contract just for vacant houses, I have the standard Realtor contract, I have the typical 2-page contracts wholesalers like to use, as well as Joint Venture agreements and all the other files I use to run my business on a daily basis. I highly recommend you check them out if you're trying to get a head start on sourcing some of these documents you'll need along the way.

Speed Is The Key

Speed is important to getting deals done. From my experience, the longer a deal takes to come together, the less likely it is to close. That's why I have an expectation for my team to process leads within 72 hours or less.

From the time we find the seller to the time we make an offer or choose to pass on the property should be 72 hours or less ideally. Occasionally the seller needs additional days to show you the property, in which case the timer continues once we view the property. Ideally from viewing to making an offer or passing should be 48 hours or less. Speed is the key. And if it is a good deal it may not be there when you get done thinking about whether it is or not.

Don't rush through steps or overlook things because you're in a hurry though. 72 hours is more than enough time to do the analysis necessary to determine your offer on a property.

Not Every Contract Becomes A Close

Once you've done your analysis and given your offer and the seller says yes, it's time to match this property to a buyer that you know is looking in that area. However, not every property you put under contract will make it to the closing table even if you're the best wholesaler out there. There are oftentimes issues that come up that prevent a deal from closing such as the taxes or a lien. Don't be discouraged though. Wholesaling is a numbers game and as long as your pipeline is stocked with potential deals, you'll have a steady deal flow coming in.

CHAPTER 6:
Marketing Like A Pro

80% of wholesaling is marketing. Marketing to buyers, marketing to sellers, marketing properties, marketing yourself.... Marketing is going to be your best friend from here on out in the funnel. In the case where you don't have a buyer but you have a property under contract, you need to find a buyer as quickly as possible.

There are tons of ways to market your property once you have it under contract. Here are some of my best strategies for getting your contracts sold:

1. Bandit Signs and Flyers
2. Craigslist.org
3. Cold Calling Buyers In The Area
4. Direct Mailing Buyers In The Area
5. Realtors
6. JV Deals
7. OfferUp
8. LetGo

9. Facebook Marketplace and Groups
10. Instagram
11. Presenting At REIA Meetings
12. Text and Email Campaigns sent to known buyers

These are just a sample of the variety of ways I like to market my properties to investors in the area. There are many more strategies as well as how to implement them in the guides located in the back of this book.

Try to use the methods in combination with one another. They work best when combined and used on a consistent daily basis. When you place your property on all these different sites and send it to your buyers in all these different ways, you get more eyes on your property. Many times the amount of impressions (or views) that a property gets determines how much it sells for and how fast. Most wholesalers are just barely scratching the surface in regards to marketing their properties.

JV Deals

My advice when it comes to JV Deals is to try to do it yourself for at least two-thirds of the contract length before you allow anyone to JV with you. There's no need in giving up half your assignment fee when you have buyers in place already and you know how to market a deal. Most times people looking to JV deals are those who went out and got a property under contract without having any buyers lined up. Keep thousands in your pocket by utilizing the other strategies in this book and selling the property yourself.

Bandit Signs and Flyers

One of the best ways to market a property is by placing bandit signs and flyers at and near the subject property. This lets local investors know you have a deal nearby and directs them to the property. You'll get many calls using this strategy. Just be sure to discern who's a real-life cash buyer and who's a wholesaler trying to bring you a buyer to the deal.

Feedback is Key

Get as many offers as you can in the early stages of the contract. Get a general sense of what investors are looking to spend on the property. If you consistently get offers that are lower than what you have the property under contract for, you should go back to the seller and try to renegotiate a lower contract price. If you need to renegotiate try to do that as early as you can as to not upset or confuse the seller. A property is only worth what someone is willing to spend on it. Your goal is to field as many offers as you can in as short a period of time as possible to gauge what the market is willing to spend.

It's A Deal

Once you've fielded offers and you know you've got an offer that allows you to give the seller what they're looking for and get paid as well, you've got a deal! Try to take the highest offer but from the most serious buyer. The last thing you want is to lock the property up with a buyer who isn't serious or doesn't have much experience investing. This can cause delays and threaten the deal's existence. Serious, active investors have a way about themselves. They know what they want and they know how much they want to spend. If you've got one of these buyers, I recommend you go with them on the deal even if you'll make a little less in your assignment fee. A buyer is not a real buyer until they've pulled the trigger on something. Most people are tire-kickers, meaning instead of actually investing, they like to think about investing and never actually take action.

Once you've got a deal and the buyer has agreed to pay you for the property you'll send them an assignment contract to sign. Once they sign the assignment contract and the seller has already signed their purchase and sale agreement, your

You're Only One Deal Away!

deal will be off to the title company! Next we'll talk about how to get the deal through the pipeline to make sure you get paid.

CHAPTER 7:
Closing & Getting Paid

Closing. The part you've been waiting for! Closing is the process is finalizing a real estate transaction. During the closing process several things take place. Most of these tasks are handled by the title company or attorney you're working with.

You're main job during the closing process is to make sure everyone is on the same page and understands what is going to happen. You'll want to make sure certain tasks are accomplished by the buyer and seller such as signing and providing documents to the title company.

Things That May Come Up

While closing a deal there are many things that can come up to prevent your deal from closing. We've talked about a few of those things but I'll list them here.

1. The seller thinks you're making too much

2. The buyer thinks you're making too much
3. Unexpected costs such as taxes, liens and violations arise during the title search
4. The buyer and/or seller are not clear about the terms of the deal and choose to back out

These are the most common reasons deals fall apart at the closing table but there are many other examples. Your most important job is to disclose all the details of the deal to everyone involved so everyone is on the same page. You're the one who brought everyone together and during closing you have to make sure everyone stays on track. Make sure everyone knows when the expected closing date is and what's required of them.

If your seller or buyer does not have an attorney you may have to connect them with one to get the deal done. You should have these connections in place already as well as the title company relationship. With your facilitators in place and communication at a peak, getting the deal through the closing process should be a breeze.

The closing process is when details about the property will be disclosed such as the official amount due for taxes, liens and violations owed on the property. These costs must be paid before the property ownership can be transferred. It is important to have an exact number or a very close estimate as to what the taxes, liens and violations amount to prior to placing the property under contract. What I like to use is a document I had my attorney create for me called the Property Financial Disclosure Agreement. This document requires the seller to provide documentation for all amounts due on the property and acts as another contingency if the numbers are inaccurate. You'll want to provide a copy of this document to your buyer before closing as well so they are aware of any amounts due.

In the case you don't get this information and it turns out there are amounts due on the property, you may have to eat those costs. You're the first one out of the deal when things arise at the closing table. Or you could end up in a situation where more than half your assignment fee is consumed by the seller's hidden tax bill. I can't tell you how often deals collapse because information wasn't disclosed before the closing. Before you place a property under contract be sure to get as much of the back story as possible and have your seller sign the Property Financial Disclosure Agreement (available in the back of this book).

As a wholesaler, you may not even been required to attend the closing to get paid. The title company or attorney will be cutting you a check for the amount you are due and you can

You're Only One Deal Away!

typically pick it up in person, have it mailed to you or get a wire transfer directly into your account. After the buyer and seller signs their paperwork, you and the seller are paid and the buyer receives the deed to their new property! You will have officially closed your first (or next) wholesale deal!

Now that you've closed one or maybe even a few at this point, it's time to start scaling up and having other do some of these processes for you.

CHAPTER 8:
Automation & Delegation

Let me start this section by saying, if you have not read the rest of this book you should NOT be starting at this portion of the book unless you've closed at least 5 deals yourself in the last 3 months. Otherwise, start from the beginning or where you left off. Many people want to start their businesses with automation from the beginning without ever learning the basics themselves. This is not a sustainable business model if you are not proficient enough at the tasks involved to know whether someone else is doing a good or not. In other words, you can't lead somewhere you've never been.

With that being said, the only way to scale a business is with the help of the right people. Great people are at the heart of every great business. I've been able to hire some amazing people onto my team and we've grown and faced struggles together that made us stronger. Added other people to your system is the best way to multiply your abilities exponentially. Let's talk about some key members you'll want to add to your wholesaling team when you're ready to start scaling.

1. Cold Callers
2. House Hunters
3. Acquisition Managers
4. Disposition Managers
5. Virtual Assistant
6. Field Guy

All of these individuals will play a major role in helping you scale your business to the next level. All of the onboarding documents to hire these people quickly and smoothly are available on my site at
https://www.edwardhayes.org/Contracts.

"But I Don't Have Money Ed"

You won't need it. Not at the beginning at least. I start all of my team members off on a commission basis. They are expected to help us close on 2-5 properties per month. Meaning the cold callers have to call at least 2 people that turn into deals, the acquisition managers must go see at least 2 properties per month that turn into deals, and so on and so forth. I do this for a reason outside of the financial savings. I want to know the person can *actually* do the job before I start paying them to waste money on leads or blow appointments. I need people on my team that are go-getters. People that *want* a commission based job and know they have what it takes.

These are the people you'll be filling your team with. Hungry go-getters that are eager to help you get deals closed. It takes time to build a great team full of winners though. Be patient and keep your eye on the prize. Get rid of people who are toxic to your work culture. Be sure to have standards they need to meet. Every person on your staff should have a number they're responsible for. That can be the number of calls, number of appointments, numbers of viewings, you name it. And when people can't perform up to standards changes must be made accordingly. The people who stay on will help you company grow to greater and greater heights.

Here's how my funnel flows: *we already have buyers in place*

1. We gather seller leads via driving for dollars, pulling lists online, internet marketing, offline marketing, etc
2. Acquisition manager get the leads skip traced in-house
3. Ringless voicemail drops are sent out on a schedule
4. Direct mail is sent to entire list
5. Cold callers start to call list and schedule appointments
6. Acquisition managers go on appointments to view and analyze properties

7. Offer is given to seller or we choose to pass
8. Disposition manager sends contract out to seller and starts to market to buyers
9. Field guy prepares property for closing and places bandit signs and lockbox
10. Disposition managers receive offers on the property, gets assignment contract signed
11. Get informed of closing date by disposition manager
12. Receive check or wire transfer from title company
13. Store all documents accordingly and pay staff from deal

This did not happen overnight! But this is the strategy I use to do 5-8 wholesale deals per month right now. At some point, if you want to scale up and start getting more deals than you could do alone, you may want to consider automating your business utilizing the strategies above. Every person should have their own system that works for them though. So do what feels right to you but know that these strategies are working for someone else and you don't have to reinvent the wheel.

CHAPTER 9:
In Conclusion

All of the strategies mentioned in this book are ones that we currently use in our business. My goal with this book is to give you an insight into how a wholesaling business operates so you can replicate my business model for yourself. I purposely made the book short and straight to the point as to remove any excess fluff. The guides, scripts and templates in the back of this book are designed to help you implement the strategies laid out in this book easily and efficiently.

Wholesaling has changed my entire life. It's allowed me to be able to spend time with the people I love and work helping other people accomplish their dreams. My hope is that you will use the tools in this book and start to take massive action towards your goals immediately.

Most importantly, I hope that you see my business model as a standard. So many "gurus" out there are teaching people to run their businesses in a disingenuous way. I can't think of another industry where the standard teachings involve lying to and deceiving people. Wholesaling has become the wild wild west and there's much room to improve standards.

We should all be running our businesses with integrity and being honest. Anyone who is teaching you to lie to and deceive others does not deserve the time of day. Share this book with others who could benefit from its contents. I hope this book has provided you with valuable content and tools you haven't heard anywhere else.

I offer coaching and mentoring services as well as an online course so if you need any additional tools or resources after completing the book, feel free to reach out to me on my website https://www.edwardhayes.org. My greatest pleasure in life is helping other people succeed. I look forward to hearing your success stories.

You've got the roadmap, now it's time to take action with what you've learned. Use the resources below to implement the strategies laid out in this book.

Happy Wholesaling!

CHAPTER 10: Guides & Resources

HOW TO FIND CASH BUYERS

Here are some of my favorite ways to find buyers

1. Local REIA Meetings
2. Craigslist.org ads
3. Facebook Groups and personal pages. Other social media sites as well
4. Instagram - search local area for hashtags #flippingchicago #fixandflip #buyinghouses #wholesaling
5. Property management companies and title companies - allow them to pass my info to anyone who's looking to buy and sell real estate
6. Insurance agents
7. Realtors
8. Word of mouth
9. Flyers and Business cards - put them everywhere, Lowes, Home Depot, Menards etc

You're Only One Deal Away!

10. Bandit Signs
11. The MLS - recent cash transactions
12. Direct mailing
13. Stickers on gas pumps - 87 button
14. Gosection8.com
15. Forrentbyowner.com
16. Motivatedsellerleads.org
17. Propstream.com
18. REWW.com

Edward Hayes

HOW TO BUILD A MASSIVE CASH BUYERS LIST

1. GoSection8.com - www.gosection8.com is a great resource to find landlords who are looking for tenants. This site works great for reaching out to some serious players in your area. You can get their contact information right there on the site in minutes.

2. Forrentbyowner.com - www.forrentbyowner.com is another great resource for reaching out to landlords who may be looking for more investments

3. Craigslist.com - www.craigslist.com - Strategy 1: When you get to Craigslist, choose your area, go to housing wanted and when you get there click the drop down menu to choose "Real Estate Wanted". Call those buyers. Strategy 2: Ghost Ads: Post a property you may or may not have on the site for sale at a great price most people can't refuse. When they call you let them know that property has sold but you can take their information down and send them curated properties based on what their looking for.

4. Facebook Ads - https://www.facebook.com/business/ads Target homeowners with incomes of 100,000 or more ages

40+. Use a captivating image or video and ask them are they looking for their next investment property

5. Freedomsoft - https://freedomsoft.com/ - Freedomsoft can be a great asset to find buyers. You have to enter your card info to get access to the buyer information however. It normally costs $200/month at the time of this writing so it's a little costly but it can be quick as well. These leads do not come with phone numbers. Choose the buyers in your target area who have purchased in the last 6 months or less.

6. MotivatedSellerLeads.org - https://www.motivatedsellerleads.org/ This is my number one recommended way to get your cash buyer leads. Simply fill out a form and receive a list of cash buyers that have purchased in your target area. Leads are as low as 12 cents per lead as of this writing.

7. REI Meetings - www.meetup.com Meetup.com can be a great place to find local REI Meetings to start meeting local investors and movers and shakers in your area. Once there be sure to interact and get as many cash buyer phone numbers as you can. Build rapport!

8. Google Ads - https://www.google.com/adsense/start/ For Google Ads use the same strategy as Facebook but have a website that they can go to. Use captivating TEXT headline to capture their attention. Use "call extensions" so they can reach out to you directly from your ad.

9. Bandit Signs & Flyers - https://www.dirtcheapsigns.com/ Use bandit signs and flyers to reach a local audience on the ground. Bandit signs should be placed as high up as possible to reduce the chance someone takes it out the ground. Also post flyers everywhere. Blanket entire areas and use signs that capture people's attention and are different (i.e. Yellow, Neon, Red Signs).

10. Direct Mail - https://click2mail.com/ You can create, customize and send your direct mail using click to mail. Postcards typically cost about 50 cents per postcard to ship to buyers.

11. Propstream - http://trial.propstreampro.com/thewholesalecoach You can do just about everything you need to run your business on Propstream actually. It's my #1

You're Only One Deal Away!

recommended tool for wholesalers. You can copy all of the buyers from a given area and add them into a Campaign. Using the campaign feature you can skip trace, direct mail and cold call your cash buyer prospects all from your online dashboard. They make it easy.

Edward Hayes

HOW TO BECOME A CONCIERGE FOR BUYERS:

Hey is this (buyer name)?

Hey (buyer name)! My name is (your name) I'm reaching out because I see you have a property on _____ and I just wanted to see if you were interested in purchasing any more properties?

They typically say "What do you have?"

Well (buyer name), the difference between me and other people in the industry is that I work as a concierge for my buyers. I can get you any property, anywhere and typically for the price you want to pay. Is it alright if I can ask you some questions so I can get out there hunting for you?

They typically say "Ok" or start telling you the types of properties they typically buy. If the latter, make sure you take detailed notes!

Here are the questions to ask. Ask them in a very conversational tone for best results. This shouldn't sound like a FBI interview!

You're Only One Deal Away!

1. So how many properties have you purchased in the last 6 months? _____ Ok so that's about _____ per month. Is that a good number of acquisitions per month for you? _____. If no, what would you like that number to be? _____

2. And how are you currently sourcing your properties? (i.e. MLS, brokers, lists, etc.)

   _____

   _____

3. What types of deals are you looking for? (rehabs, buy and holds, personal use, etc..)

   _____

   _____

4. What's your preferred price range for a property and how much are you typically looking to make back on your investment?

   _____

5. And what areas do you most prefer if you could choose any where?

_____

_____

6. What areas do you like to stay away from?

_____

_____

7. What types of properties are you most interested in? (i.e. single family, multi, mobile etc.)

_____

_____

8. And how many beds, baths and square footage are you looking for?

_____

9. Ok, and are you buying them cash or financing?

_____

_____

10. If I were to bring you something that matches the criteria you've given me, what's the quickest you'd be able to close on the property?

_____

_____

"Ok great. So a little bit more about me (buyer name). As I said earlier, I work as a concierge for my buyers. I like to provide customized solutions to my buyers and essentially become a part of your team. I want to be the person that you go to when you want a new property in a certain area. I'm like a marketing machine. Now that I have your criteria I'm going to put out as many nets as possible to bring you what you're looking for. I don't wanna bore with all the details but I make a ton of cold calls and I have house hunters and I advertise online just to name a few methods. But I may reach out to you before I put something under contract just to make sure it's something you'd move on. How's that sound?

And always, if there are certain areas or certain types of properties you want besides what you've told me today definitely feel free to reach out to me. I love finding those hidden gems no one else can seem to get.

They respond with enthusiasm usually

11. Ok awesome, I think I've got most of what I need here (buyer name). Can I have the best email address for you?

_____

_____

12. And is this the best phone number to reach you at? No? _____

Ok perfect. Alright (buyer name) I'll go ahead and let you go, thank you so much for taking my call and I'm looking forward to talking to you soon with some potential deals for you to check out! Alright (buyer name), have a great one :)

You're Only One Deal Away!

Enter all information gathered into an online database for safe keeping. Start hunting immediately if motivation level was high. Get something for them within 7-14 days of talking to them for best results. Add any additional questions that you feel necessary. Be conversational!

COMPILING A LIST OF MOTIVATED SELLERS

Here are my favorite ways (that I'm using currently) to find motivated sellers in the areas my buyers are looking in:

1. Driving for Dollars - Driving for dollars is probably the best way to find motivated seller leads. You drive around the community looking for vacant and distressed properties. You can alternatively hire house hunters who can go out and find these properties for you on a commission basis. Here are my strategies for driving for dollars

2. Bandit Signs/Flyers - Bandit signs and flyers can be a great way to generate some leads if you're targeting small to medium sized areas. Make sure your flyers stand out with different colors and/or headlines. You'll want to post 100's of flyers and at least 50 bandit signs to generate a good amount of phone traffic.

3. MotivatedSellerLeads.org - https://www.motivatedsellerleads.org/ This is my number one recommended way to get your motivated seller leads quickly. Simply fill out a form and receive a

list of motivated seller leads in your target area. Leads are as low as 12 cents per lead as of this writing.

4. Propstream - Propstream is an all-in-one system to help to find leads, skip trace their numbers, direct mail and call them all from one platform. If you're interested in beginning with Propstream here is a 7-day free trial. You can search the areas your buyers are buying in and download entire lists of different types of distressed sellers.

5. Facebook Ads –
https://www.facebook.com/business/ads

Target homeowners 55+ that indicate they are moving or going through divorce or have a recently deceased parent. Use a captivating image or video and ask them do they need to sell their home quickly for whatever reason.

6. Google Ads –
https://www.google.com/adsense/start/

For Google Ads use the same strategy as Facebook but have a website that they can go to. Use captivating TEXT headline to capture their attention. Use "call extensions" so they can reach out to you directly from your ad.

7. Public Records - The most massive lists of leads can be found by searching public records. Check your county websites (search "pre-foreclosure (your county), tax delinquent (your county)) to find the relevant county websites. In some area you may have to go the county courthouse to obtain the list you are looking for.

8. Direct Mail - Using click to mail you can send out a massive list of postcards to your sellers. However, an even better strategy is to send your list some "lumpy mail" which is a self-addressed envelope containing your business flyer (with an optional picture of yourself on it), and a business card inside and/or something else that causes the receiver to notice there is something inside of the envelope. They almost always open it!

9. Facebook and Instagram Organic Reach - You don't HAVE to spend money to run ads on Facebook and Instagram but you SHOULD. If you choose the free route for now, then I would recommend creating a content calendar for yourself to make sure you have constant content being released to your audience. Over time this audience will grow and can retarget all

the people that engaged with your organic content with paid advertisements.

10. Local advertising/Collaborating - Considering linking up with other community leaders to do things for the community. Make sure your local neighbors know who you are. Get to know them using mini-events and pop-up meetings. Find a local business owner who will allow you host meetings to teach people how to get financially literate and save their homes. (This will build genuine trust in the community and solidify you as the clear choice if/when they do decide to sell)

11. Underpriced FSBO's - Reach out to For Sale by Owner ads on Realtor.com, redfin.com, trulia.com, Zillow.com, and Craigslist.com. Everyday contact at least 50 sellers by phone or email and offer them a portion (maybe 60%) of what they're asking for. *Always analyze numbers beforehand to know it makes sense.

12. Blogging - A blog can be a little thought of, but very strategic way to bring in motivated sellers who need to sell their homes. You'll want to stock this blog with plenty of helpful tips for homeowners in your target

area. (i.e. articles titled "How to sell my Atlanta foreclosure")

13. Referrals/Word of Mouth - Some of the most consistent leads will come from repeat business and word of mouth from happy clients and people who have seen your marketing over a period of time. Never burn any bridges, it's a small world.

COLD CALLING TIPS AND STRATEGIES

Here is a list of my favorite cold calling strategies and tips that I use every time I get on the phone. I've been cold calling for quite some time now so these are the tips that I intuitively understand and utilize without having to think about and I have seen work for me in the past.

This list will not be exhaustive. There is no one perfect way to make cold calls. What matters most is that you be natural and you build a connection with the seller. Let's get right into it:

1. Smiling - When you smile on the phone you exude that energy over the phone.
    a. They can feel your positive energy
    b. You're letting them know that you're a trustworthy person
    c. You sound like someone who's happy to talk to them
    d. It's hard to feel nervous when you smile

2. Mirroring - When talking to people make sure that you remind them of themselves
    a. If they talk fast you talk fast
    b. If they talk slow paced you talk slow paced

    c. Talk like them and have the same mannerisms

    d. People like to do business with people that remind them of themselves!

3. Be Yourself - No one wants to talk to a robot.
    a. Remember you're calling them to put money in their pockets
    b. You don't have to sound extra professional or too salesly, you just want to be you.
    c. Trust in your training and know they're just another person on the phone.

4. Feel Confident - People can feel your nervousness through the phone.
    a. You have to mentally believe that you're the person who can change things for the caller. You have to be confident of your capabilities. People will feel your confidence and trust in you
    b. You're adding value to their lives - DON'T PANIC
    c. Take risks, get bold if necessary

5. Be patient and understanding - After calling 100 people and getting cursed out a few times you may feel a little disgruntled. Don't allow that emotion to slip onto the phone call with your next lead.

You're Only One Deal Away!

    a. Keep your emotions in check

    b. Understand it's in everyone's best interest to try to get the most money they can for their property and try to buy it for as low as possible. Don't take offense to this, it's business, not personal.

6. They don't hurt! - Make the calls. The worst thing that can happen is they say no. Don't be afraid to put yourself out there. Take risks when on the phone. The most important thing you can be doing if you're a wholesaler is making contacts with sellers and buyers.

7. Conversion Numbers matter - We're in a business where our conversion rate may be 1-5%. You need to make a ton of calls if you want to get paid. Make sure you enjoy the process and stay consistent. You're going to face a lot of rejection but you have to keep going. Those conversion numbers matter. Think every 300 calls made MAY turn into 1-2 deals

8. Deep dive into problems - Listen to what their saying on the phone. When they tell you about specifics issues they're dealing with, ask them to tell you more about it. Be relatable and interested in what they have going on.

Here are some common objections or questions and how to overcome them:

1. How did you get my phone number?
    a. I use a service online that gives me the numbers to places I'm interested in… so I figured I'd reach out to you to see if you were interested in selling. (Always divert back to the reason why you called)

2. What's your offer? (Before you see go out to see the place)
    a. Well, I'd like to get you an offer on the property, but I need to know more about it. If you have a few minutes I'd like to ask you a few questions about the property so I can get you a legitimate offer. Is that okay?

3. What's your business name or website (When you don't have one)
    a. This is one you're gonna have to tackle beforehand. One good way to get established online is to buy your domain name (.com) then get an email address that goes along with that (you@yourbusinessname.com). Set up a quick

website on Wordpress or Google Sites for free. Connect your domain name to your new website and have your business email listed on the site. Viola!

4. Earnest money question
   a. A lot of times if their asking for earnest money they aren't very motivated to begin with.

   b. But if you had to put some money down I would put down between $10-$100.

   c. If you don't have any money to put down what i'd tell them is "We don't put earnest money down because we close quickly and we're paying with cash. We can lock this up quickly if you're still interested."

   d. Your best bet is not to mention anything about earnest money. Many times they don't know what that is and don't care.

   e. Keep in mind some title companies may require you to deposit a certain amount of earnest money to process the transaction.

COLD CALLER INTERVIEW FLOW

Intro:
1. Let them know you'll be telling them more about the business, what the job actually entails, find out a little more about them and going from there
2. Introduce yourself as a real estate investor and let them know you're building your team.

The business:
1. Ask if they know what wholesaling is and if their familiar with it
    a. If not, break it down
2. Explain the flow of wholesaling (lead comes in, they take the call, pass it on to REAMS or you, then it gets slammed dunk)

What the job entails:
1. Making calls to motivated home owners
2. Building rapport and gathering vital information about property
3. Scheduling viewings
4. Updated your list using our CRM

5. Passing information collected from talking to sellers to your acquisition manager or (you)
6. Making 50-200 calls per day is the quota
7. Help us close on 2 properties per month
8. Work from home, remote job
9. Access to Propstream (and Asana)
10. Google Voice phone number to make calls from
11. Commission is as follows: $1,000 per deal flat fee for the first 2 deals or 30 days we close on and we expect our callers to help us close on 2+ properties per month. After 30 days we can discuss a base pay plus commission.
12. You can do this in your spare time or part time

Ask them if that sounds good to them. Answer any followup questions

Ask them to tell you about themselves and what experience they have that may be relevant to the position. They will give you info. Pay attention to the answer to the questions below. Only ask if they don't tell you this stuff voluntarily.

Find out about them:
1. How long have they been cold calling
2. Do they feel comfortable calling homeowners (if it's different from what they've done in the past)

3. Do they have a comfortable place in their house to make these calls
4. Are they *really* comfortable with the job (give them outs, you only want people that really want the job)
5. What does their current schedule look like (are they working? If so, what are their hours)
6. Do you think you can make 50-200 calls per day?
7. When would be the soonest they would be able to start if you both decided to move forward?

What happens next:
1. We still have other candidates that we are reviewing right now so we will definitely be getting back to you soon
2. When is a good time for you to have another interview possibly in the next few days?
3. Schedule a time to interview them again if interested
4. In the next interview we'll hop on a practice call or two and go through the seller lead sheet to make sure you feel comfortable over the phone.
5. We'll send over the script and the seller lead sheet in advance so you're prepared for the call.

Second interview:

You're Only One Deal Away!

On the second interview you're going to want to see whether they can actually do the job or not.

1. Ask if they have any questions about the last interview or anything moving forward.
2. Answer any questions they may have
3. Have a few leads ready to call
4. Ask them if they've reviewed the lead sheet and script
5. Have them role play with you a couple times to gauge their comfortability over the phone
6. Call some sellers and chime them in on 3 way
7. Let them begin to talk to the seller and see how they handle the call
8. Gauge their abilities based using this scale: (add your own categories as needed)
    i. Confidence over the phone (1-5)_____
    ii. Articulation (1-5) _____
    iii. Clearly states reason for call (1-5) _____
    iv. Asks vital questions (1-5) _____
    v. Schedules appointment (10 bonus points) _____
    vi. Composure throughout call (1-5) _____

9. Evaluate their call and provide feedback to them to help them on the next call
10. Ask if they are still interested and when would they be ready to start making calls
11. Schedule a time for them to start making calls
12. Let them know you will be sending them some leads and some onboarding information (Propstream login info, Calendly link in an email sent to them after the call, and the independent contractor agreement)

After the call:
1. Send welcome email and contract
2. Receive contract back
3. Then send Propstream login info, Asana login info, Calendly link, leads to start calling on a Google Drive link
4. Follow up with them daily starting the day they can begin working.
5. Make sure they input all lead information into asana and color code Google Sheets daily

You're Only One Deal Away!

In-Person Meeting With Motivated Seller Meeting Checklist

- ❏ Market Research (Tax Records /Comps)
- ❏ 2 Pens
- ❏ Notebook or Yellow
- ❏ Notepad - Take note of anything wrong with the property
- ❏ 2 Purchase and Sale Agreements
- ❏ Smartphone (Camera /Calculator)
- ❏ Get Great video of entire inside of property
- ❏ Get pictures of entire inside of property
- ❏ Get pictures of entire outside of property (front, side, back)
- ❏ Foundation condition
- ❏ Roof Condition
- ❏ Kitchen/Bath Condition
- ❏ Windows and Flooring Condition
- ❏ Furnace and Hot water heater Condition

39 DIFFERENT WAYS TO MARKET YOUR WHOLESALING BUSINESS

1. Direct mail postcards
2. Direct mail yellow letters
3. Direct mail printed letter w/pictures and business card in it
4. Business Cards
5. Flyers
6. Stickers
7. Bandit Signs
8. Website
9. Google Ads (run heavy if in small area, do better if in big)
10. Facebook Ads (run heavy if in small area, do better if in big)
11. Going to rei meetings
12. Meeting with cash buyers, realtors and wholesalers in person to get to know them
13. Craigslist Ads
14. Facebook Marketplace and Groups
15. OfferUp app
16. LetGo app
17. Google my business
18. Blogging
19. Leave business cards at local businesses

20. Car Magnets
21. Wholesaling swag (hoodies, t-shirts etc...)
22. House Hunters
23. Cold Callers
24. Power dialing using dialers like Mojo
25. Add 100 buyers to your list in one month
26. Add 20 realtors to your list
27. Start a local rei meeting
28. Ask to speak at a school
29. Ask to speak at a community gathering (rebuilding communities)
30. Door knocking
31. Enlist the mail people to become your house hunters for commission
32. Don't be afraid to personally reach out to the power players and ask for help
33. Lock arms with other wholesalers in your area to create more uniformity and integrity
34. Door hangers
35. Newspaper ad depending on your area
36. Pens
37. Calendars
38. Radio Ads
39. Partnerships with other well known figures in the community - collaborations

HOW TO SKIP TRACE ONLINE FREE

If you'd prefer to watch that instead/as well here is the link: https://www.youtube.com/watch?v=-UcuhxBJatI it will supplement this content well.

1. TruePeopleSearch - My favorite website to skip trace leads on is https://www.truepeoplesearch.com/. You simply do a reverse address lookup (if you already have the address) or do a name search if you only have their name. Once you find the correct person simply copy and paste the phone numbers into your spreadsheet under the "Phone" column.

2. FastPeopleSearch - Process is basically the same is Truepeoplesearch. Either do a reverse address lookup or a name search and find the correct person. Once you find them simply copy and paste their phone numbers into your spreadsheet under the "Phone" column. https://fastpeoplesearch.com

3. Fiverr Consultants - Use of a Fiverr may be key if you don't have much time to skip trace these leads yourself. I typically between 10-25 cents per lead when getting leads skip traced by Fiverr consultants. I now

only use in-house skip tracing using True People Search though.

4. Intellius - This is the option you want to use if you want to have the ability to skip trace while on the move. Intellius has a sleek user interface and costs about $9.99/month. However, I would still recommend True People Search since it's free and you can still use it on your phone.

5. Been Verified - Lastly, BeenVerified is another long-established leader in the "finding people" industry. However unless you want to pay for their membership fees, you'll have to sit through really long waiting screens just to be told to put in your contact info, then they still only give you a brief snapshot. However if you get their paid service, the results are pretty good.

Edward Hayes

** CATCHY HEADLINE THAT GRABS THEIR ATTENTION!!! ***

Full Property Address or 1xx Main St, City State Zip

Quick Intro statement. Get personal. Address this area to the individual buyer. Brief summary of the property situation and ARV (Example: Owner purchased this property at an auction and just wants to get rid of it. Don't miss out on this deal!! Legit comps for the area are about $83k! (Comps attached to this email). GREAT RENTAL PROPERTY)

Asking Price: $xx,xxx

Beds and Baths

Sq. Ft

Sq. Ft. Lot

Rental Estimate

Occupancy:

You're Only One Deal Away!

Construction:

Land Use:

Basement:

Estimated Taxes:

Comps: (Attached to this email) Avg Sale Price $xx,xxx
Avg Days On Market:

If you or anyone you know may be interested in this property reach out to me via phone, text or email. This one won't last long! To schedule a viewing or for more info contact me right away.

Talk soon!

Phone: xxx-xxx-xxxx   Email: example@example.com

Edward Hayes

THE WHOLESALING CHECKLIST

Relationship Building:

- ❏ Cash Buyers (Craigslist, REWW, ReiPro, REI Meetings)
- ❏ Realtors (Comps, Pocket Listings, Expired Listings, Cash Buyers)
- ❏ Title Company/Real Estate Attorney
- ❏ Other Wholesalers
- ❏ Speak to and build up relationships with all these people *first*

Tools:

- ❏ CRM (Asana)
- ❏ Google Calendar
- ❏ Money Phone (Google Voice)
- ❏ Dialer (Mojo Dialer)
- ❏ Website Services (Kartra, Outlook Email, GoDaddy)
- ❏ Lead Generation (ReiPro, REWW, Public Records)
- ❏ Databases (Tax assessor, recorder of deeds, treasurer, code enforcement)
- ❏ Personal Smartphone (with ability to download apps)
- ❏ Computer (Laptop preferably, but desktop suffices)
- ❏ Printer

You're Only One Deal Away!

- ❏ Envelopes and Stamps
- ❏ Business Cards
- ❏ Docusign App
- ❏ Landglide App

Team Building:

- ❏ Cold Callers (1-2 people calling at least 100 people per day)
- ❏ Acquisition Managers (3-4 local people that can go see properties when needed)
- ❏ House Hunters (5-10 people who will send you vacant and distressed property addresses)
- ❏ You (You can be all of these people at the beginning and/or when necessary)

Lead Generation:

- ❏ Lists from List Brokers (ReiPro, REWW)
- ❏ Public Records *see databases above*
- ❏ Bandit Signs (Put out 50 every Friday, pick up Sunday)
- ❏ Flyers (Put out 50 every 2 weeks in libraries, currency exchanges, anywhere else where it's legal)
- ❏ Business Cards (leave at businesses, drop in your direct mail envelopes, give to people)
- ❏ Facebook Ads

- ❏ Car Banner/Magnet
- ❏ Direct Mail (Postcards, Enveloped letters)
- ❏ House Hunters
- ❏ Craigslist Ghost Ads

Lead Acquisition:

- ❏ Cold Callers (Outbound - Call sellers, build rapport, get lead sheets, set up callbacks or perform warm transfers, min.100 call/day)
- ❏ Inbound Call Takers (Typically your Closers)
- ❏ Seperate Google Voice Numbers
- ❏ REI(A) Meetings
- ❏ Networking Events
- ❏ Inside Referrals (house hunters, cold callers, realtor leads)
- ❏ CRM (Use Asana to organize and manage all new leads coming in)
- ❏ Closers (1-2 people to get on the phone and get the deal signed)
- ❏ Facebook Posts (groups, personal pages, ads)
- ❏ Craigslist (FSBO, houses for rent, real estate wanted)
- ❏ GoSection8, Forrentbyowner
- ❏ Zillow, Realtor.com, Trulia, Redfin, Craigslist (For Sale By Owner Ads)
- ❏ Skip Tracing (Fiverr Consultants, ReiSkip, Landglide)

- ❏ Reach out to family and friends looking to sell and/or invest
- ❏ Sending handwritten letters to people in high distress situations (tax delinquent, pre-foreclosure) and put business card in envelope
- ❏ Sending postcards through Click2Mail
- ❏ Send direct mail to probate and divorce attorneys telling them you specialize in those properties and would love to work with them
- ❏ Higher distress = Higher likelihood of being a deal

Property Inspection/Evaluation:

- ❏ Set up time to go meet seller or their representative at the property
- ❏ Take a camera, flashlight, long sleeved shirt, pants, another person with you preferably if it's vacant, paper and pen to take notes, and a cell phone
- ❏ Make sure property is in decent shape depending on what buyers are looking for (light rehab + low-cost = winning situation)
- ❏ Get a great video of entire property, every square inch and pictures of entire property (2 rounds through house is needed)
- ❏ Take notes on anything specific that you see needs to be repaired and may be expensive

- ❏ Look for mold damage, old/damaged roof, holes in walls/floors, structural damage
- ❏ Send address over to realtor for comps when leads comes in from Caller
- ❏ Verify property is in a reasonable area and the seller is not asking for an unreasonable price
- ❏ Upload videos and pics to a Google Drive link
- ❏ Post Google Drive link in Asana under the lead
- ❏ The numbers MUST MAKE SENSE - if they don't, just walk away and keep it moving
- ❏ 50-70% of a Valid ARV - repair costs - your assignment fee = MAO
- ❏ Using this formula many properties should be priced around the 40-50% of ARV mark or less. In other words, you want to be buying the property for 40-50% of what it will be worth after you rehab it or less. This is generally good depending on the property

Lead Disposition:

- ❏ Calling Cash Buyers with already established relationships and following up with cash buyers through email, text, voicemail

You're Only One Deal Away!

- ❏ Calling brand new cash buyers through Craigslist, REWW, ReiPro
- ❏ Going to REI Meetings and shopping the deal
- ❏ Creating buyer packages with relevant info about the property included (send this whenever people ask for extra info about the property)
- ❏ Creating unique bit.ly links for the Google Drive link containing pics and videos
- ❏ Know the comps, specific neighborhood, sq. ft., beds and baths, repair estimates and what needs to be done when you get these buyers on the phone, they'll ask questions!
- ❏ Talk to at least 20-50 buyers a day when trying to sell the property
- ❏ Take in feedback and criticism about the property to make any necessary adjustments to the marketing or renegotiating the sales price
- ❏ Market property online (Craigslist, OfferUp, LetGo, Facebook Marketplace and Groups, your personal website, Email)
- ❏ Let family, friends and acquaintances know you have properties for sale
- ❏ Lower price accordingly when property hasn't sold at current price for 14 days or more
- ❏ Post bandit signs at and near the subject property with "Investor Special" on them (2-5)

- Post flyers near subject properties in all public areas where legal
- Send direct mail to buyers telling them you have other investment properties they may be interested in (put business card in envelope)
- Send ad traffic to your "properties" page (targeting cash buyers)
- Have a full-on team effort to dispose of properties (everybody focuses on a different stream so as not to confuse any buyers)(online, over the phone, on the ground)
- Try to always be direct to your own cash buyers
- When JV is necessary, be sure to get it in writing
- Have a chief negotiator/decision maker who chooses to either close on the deal, renegotiate or pass on the deal when necessary
- Be consistent with following up with buyers, leave voicemails and let them know not to waste your time
- Commit to getting a yes or no from your buyers within 7 days or less from the time you send them the deal.
- Require earnest money deposit from every buyer you deal with
- Ask realtor friends if they have any buyers for the properties you have
- Don't fall in love with the property… Fall in love with the numbers!

You're Only One Deal Away!

Daily Acquisition Duties:

- ❏ Cold Call at least 100 Motivated Sellers daily
- ❏ Go Driving for Dollars at least once weekly in different neighborhoods
- ❏ Have house hunters looking for vacant houses throughout target areas (follow up with them weekly with updates on their properties)
- ❏ Get leads skip traced bi-weekly or all at once for the month
- ❏ Post 50 flyers every Wednesday in different neighborhoods
- ❏ Post 50 bandit signs up on Friday and pick up on Sunday
- ❏ Compile all new leads to be skip traced onto spreadsheet daily
- ❏ Update new information about leads into Asana daily
- ❏ Look for and call new FSBO leads every Monday
- ❏ Compile and "clean up" lists from public records daily to be skip traced bi-weekly (minimum 100 weekly added to skip trace list)
- ❏ Write 50+ handwritten letters to people on high distressed lists and people that asked for mail to be sent to them monthly (have picture of yourself on letter and business card inside envelope)

- Answer every inbound call within 2 rings and answer with a business greeting (use a script)
- Make sure house hunters are looking for properties (add these leads into spreadsheet for skip tracing daily/as they come in). Always be hiring more hunters
- Go to networking events and REI Meetings 2-3 times monthly to get the latest insights into the market and network with other investors
- Distribute business cards efficiently for maximum exposure
- Build new list for cold calling once weekly from ReiPro, REWW ~2500 leads/week
- Once weekly compile ALL LEADS (house hunting, public records and the rest ReiPro/REWW) to get skip traced ~500 leads/week

Daily Disposition Duties:

- Call/Follow up with at least 20-50 potential cash buyers daily when deals are on the line
- Post bandit signs at/near properties under contract
- Create buyer packages using proven formats and accurate information
- Call cash buyers from ReiPro and REWW who have properties where our subject properties are located

You're Only One Deal Away!

- ❏ Go to REI Meetings and networking events 2-3 times monthly to get to know cash buyers personally
- ❏ Once weekly try to have a sit-down conversation/face-to-face meeting with a cash buyer to get to know them better and establish a relationship (starbucks maybe, you pay)
- ❏ Place all new properties on "properties" page on website daily
- ❏ Post all properties on Offer Up, Let Go, Facebook Marketplace and groups, and Craigslist
- ❏ Follow up with at least 10-20 potential cash buyers online daily when deals are on the line
- ❏ Reach out to family members, friends, acquaintances, and more to let them know about the properties you have for sale
- ❏ Receive and report any feedback and/or criticisms from potential buyers about current inventory (update Asana with that information about that lead)
- ❏ Suggest price drop for properties in pipeline for 2 weeks or more
- ❏ Place flyers for cash buyers (same day seller flyers are placed)
- ❏ Have 3 distinct disposition units: Over the phone, online, and on the ground
- ❏ Get JV contracts signed

- ❏ Send 50+ direct mail pieces out to cash buyers monthly letting them we have investment properties they may be interested in (place business card inside envelope and pic on letter)
- ❏ Update Asana with any information about these cash buyers daily. Keep records on the things they told you to be more efficient the next time you approach them
- ❏ Make sure Acquisition Managers are going out to see properties when needed

ED'S HIERARCHY OF WHOLESALING:

Foundation: ONLINE PRESENCE - SOCIAL MEDIA, WEBSITE, FORMS, OFFLINE PRESENCE - BUSINESS CARDS, FLYERS, SEPERATE PHONE NUMBER, LOGO, LLC, T-SHIRTS, BASIC UNDERSTANDING

Relationships: BUYERS, TITLE COMPANIES, ATTORNIES, REIA MEETINGS, WHOLESALERS, CONTRACTORS

Marketing: TALKING TO SELLERS, BANDIT SIGNS, DRIVING FOR DOLLARS, SKIP TRACING, DIRECT MAIL, WEBSITES, TEXT MESSAGING, EMAIL, SYSTEMS

Matchmaking: NEGOTIATING, VIEWING PROPERTIES, NOTICING DISCREPANCIES, PACKAGING YOUR DEALS, SIGNING CONTRACTS, CLOSING DEALS

Time Leveraging/Outsourcing: SKIP TRACING, SENDING DIRECT MAIL, DRIVING FOR DOLLARS, VIEWING PROPERTIES, MARKETING PROPERTIES, COLD CALLING

Delegation & Automation: RINGLESS VOICEMAIL, COLD CALLERS, ACQUISITION MANAGERS, FIELD GUYS, DIRECT MAIL, DISPOSITION MANAGERS

There are so many pieces to the wholesaling hierarchy and when you realize it's true value you'll be shocked that you weren't taught this way the first time.

First off, the leads. If you're gonna make money you're gonna need to be on the phone with the people that can make a difference in your bank account and that's buyers and sellers. You don't want just any leads though. You want fresh up to date leads that actually get you the results you're looking for. Cash buyers who've purchased in the last 6 months. Sellers in distressed situations that are much more likely to want to sell.

Then you're gonna need to get their contact information. So let's say you go out and go walk or drive around your community and you find a vacant house. That could be a potential wholesale deal. So what do you do? You go and try to get the home owner's phone number. Depending on your area this can be difficult to do, but it must be done. So getting accurate data to go along with your list is extra important.

So building your foundation is critical to mission success a lot of times in wholesaling. You want to start to create a presence online. This is the time where you decide whether you want to get an LLC or not. This is when you'll set up your website and get business cards and flyers. You'll also clean your social media profiles of everything that can harm you from getting deals. You'll decide whether you want to create a website using the free and paid services out there. People need to know who you are and you have to look credible even if you're just starting. People have all types of distrust of wholesalers. You need to establish yourself in the market as a go-to person or at least someone competent enough to get the job done.

Be sure to get adequate training and knowledge about wholesaling before taking action. You don't want to be put on the spot and can't confidently respond back to something that you should have known like "what's the ARV?". Be sure to study enough and feel confident before you even go into the next step.

Relationships are the most critical aspect of getting deals done SMOOTHLY. If you establish these relationships and do your due diligence in advance your wholesaling career will be nice and easy. You'll be able to simply call and text actual players in your local real estate market for advice or to do deals with them. WIthout these relationships you're simply hoping and wishing to get deals done. You probably don't know the actual process and you're likely lying to sellers about having buyers or being the buyer. This is the most fundamental piece to the hierarchy and typically what most wholesalers fail to even consider. Most people were taught backwards.

Once you've established your buyer's criteria it's time to start marketing to get phones ringing and help some sellers sell their homes! At this point, you want to be doing all of this yourself if possible. Do everything you can unless you absolutely have no time, in which case you'll try to hire a cold caller and/or some house hunters onto your team. But if this is the case you may want to really consider whether this is right for you or not. A business takes time to grow and when you're trying to scale from day one it's just really really hard to do. People aren't going to mesh the first or second time around. If you're in it to get out of something else that you're doing you may have to consider leaving the other thing behind or focusing on wholesaling in your spare time until you can fully commit yourself.

Start marketing in the areas that your buyers are looking for. Start calling, direct mailing, skip tracing info, flyers, bandit signs, whatever marketing strategies you decide to use. Just make sure you do them consistently and effectively. It can't be a one-time event. If you stop marketing people will forget about you. You must stay in their awareness. Use all the methods at your disposal and maximize the ones that work best. Never stop marketing!

Now that you've got some property owners interested in selling you need to put it all together. That's when you shoot the property out to your buyers and ask them how much they would be willing to spend for it. Then just simply get it under contract for less than that. You don't need to overthink or over analyze the numbers. A lot of times your buyer won't care about your numbers or will get so caught up in trying to prove your numbers wrong that you can't sell them the property. A property is only worth what someone is willing to pay for it. Never fall in love with the property. Fall in love with the numbers. If the numbers make sense, put the property under contract and get your assignment contract signed as well. Send all these documents to the title company or attorney to start the closing process. Coordinate with title company and attorney to ensure the deal goes through. Get paid.

Now it's time to wash rinse and repeat the process. You'll want to start leveraging the time of others to help you get some of your tasks done. This should decrease the amount of time it takes to get your second deal. You may want to bring in people to do your skip tracing, cold calling, and driving for dollars. You may want to hire someone to post ads on Craigslist and someone for scheduling and viewing properties. Make sure that you don't give up too much control too fast or put your business in the hands of anyone else that isn't going to care about it like you. Hire cold callers from Indeed.com. Hire house hunters from Craigslist. Hire acquisition managers from either. Pay commission or pay per job.

Eventually take yourself out the business so you can focus on bringing in more sales and opportunities for the business. It should be your job to recruit and hire new people to have the perfect "box" of people to get the job done.

HOPE THIS HELPS!!

ABOUT THE AUTHOR

Edward Hayes is a millennial real estate investor, author and entrepreneur from Chicago, Illinois. He has built multiple six-figure businesses and enjoys giving back to his community. He is known online as The Wholesale Coach and has hundreds of wholesalers across the United States get deals. To get access to all of his tools and resources or for one on one mentorship go to https://www.edwardhayes.org.

CONNECT WITH THE WHOLESALE COACH ONLINE:

MAIN SITE: https://www.edwardhayes.org

JOIN THE WHOLESALERS HUB:
https://www.edwardhayes.org/hub

LISTEN TO THE PODCAST: https://www.anchor.fm/eed

SUBSCRIBE TO THE YOUTUBE CHANNEL:
https://www.youtube.com/user/09fooman

LIKE THE FACEBOOK PAGE:
https://www.facebook.com/TheWholesaleCoach/

FOLLOW ON INSTAGRAM:
https://www.instagram.com/thewholesalecoach

www.ingramcontent.com/pod-product-compliance
Lightning Source LLC
Chambersburg PA
CBHW072156170526
45158CB00004BA/1669